Secrets of Success for Women

Time

*Practical direction and tips for women on
making the most of God's precious gift of time*

KAREN H WHITING

LIVING
INK
BOOKS
Writing Worth Reading

AMG Publishers
6815 Shallowford Road
Chattanooga
Tenessee 37421

Copyright © 2004 John Hunt Publishing Ltd

Text: © 2004 Karen Whiting

Designed by
ANDREW MILNE DESIGN

ISBN 0-89957-124-7

Scripture taken from the HOLY BIBLE,
NEW INTERNATIONAL VERSION " 1973, 1978, 1984, by
International Bible Society. Used by permission of
Zondervan Publishing House. All rights reserved

The rights of Karen Whiting as author have been
asserted in accordance with the Copyright, Designs
and Patents Act 1988.

Printed by South China Printing Company,
China

CONTENTS

4-5 Time

6-7 Jesus and time

8-9 God and time

10-11 Making the most of time with God

12-13 Goal setting

14-15 Evaluate your time

16-17 Time considerations

18-19 Consider the cost

20-21 Consider the motives

22-23 Consider the importance: prioritize

24-25 Saying "No" graciously

26-27 When to say "Yes"

28-29 Looking ahead

30-31 Accountability partner

32-33 Delegating

34-35 Time and personality

36-37 Time and hospitality

38-45 Seven successful S's when overwhelmed

Scripture support

Seek guidance

Sort it out

Simplify

Schedule time periods

Share the load

Stop to relieve stress

46-47 Overcoming procrastination

48-49 Balancing time

50-51 "Too tired" syndrome

52-53 Interruptions, disruptions, and divine appointments

54-55 Time wasters

56-57 Family time

58-59 Timely home management

60-61 Avoid time crunches on special days

62-63 Time for joy

64 Timely Scriptures

Time

God created time and set the earth in motion, giving us 24 hours each day. Time is God's gift to us. When spent wisely, there is ample time for nurturing relationships, fulfilling dreams, and experiencing joy.

God plans for each woman as he forms her. He does not give a woman more do to than humanly possible.

"For I know the plans I have for you," declares the Lord, "plans to prosper you and not to harm you, plans to give you hope and a future." Jeremiah 29:11

YOU KNOW YOU ARE OVER-COMMITTED WHEN...

You cannot get an average of 8 hours rest in a 24-hour day.

You do not have time to sit and eat with your family.

A small interruption is a major problem.

You are too impatient while driving because you are running late.

You forget to pay bills.

You have piles of mail and laundry left undone.

You have no time to sit and chat with your spouse
 or children.
You cannot recall the last time you sat and relaxed
 with a friend.
You missed an appointment.
You lost something due to lack of time to put it in
 its proper place.
You feel like life has no joy.

Too much promised for the hours over-commits the
 time. We cannot create more minutes or days.

A LIFESTYLE OF CONTINUED OVER-COMMITMENT
 CAUSES PROBLEMS THAT INCLUDE:
 Health problems, such as heart attacks
 Failure or feelings of failure
 Stress
 Anger and other emotional
  outbursts
 Broken relationships
 Depression
 Guilt over things uncompleted
  or poorly done

"Moment by moment I'm
 kept in his love
Moment by moment I've
 help from above
Looking to Jesus, till glory
 doeth shine;
Moment by moment, O
 Lord, I am thine."
 D H Whittle

To relieve the problems we must
 change how we choose to
 spend our time.

In his heart a man plans his course,
but the LORD determines his steps. Proverbs 16:9

Jesus and time

How Jesus spent his time:

JESUS TOOK TIME TO PRAY
> Early in the day (*Mark 1:35*)
> Late at night (*Luke 6:12; 22:41*)
> Before a miracle (*John 6:11*)
> At the moment he died (*Luke 23:46*)
> With others (*Luke 4:16*)

JESUS SPENT TIME IN HIS WORK OF PREACHING AND HEALING
> He healed all who came to him – that was his job. (*Matthew 4:23*)
> He multi-tasked and used the time to teach also.

HE TOOK TIME FOR SOCIAL GATHERINGS
> Attended a wedding (*John 2:1-10*)
> Enjoyed banquets and meals. (*John 6:11-14; 12:1-2*)

JESUS RESTED AND SPENT TIME WITH HIS FRIENDS.
Jesus spent time alone with friends, sometimes explaining parables, sometimes resting. (*John 3:22; Mark 6:30-31*)
> He sang with his friends. (*Matthew 26:30*)

HE TOOK TIME TO GRIEVE
He went away after the death of John the Baptist. (*Matthew 14:13*)

Decisions of Jesus regarding time

JESUS SAID "NO" TO SOME CHOICES OF USING HIS TIME WISELY.

He would not perform signs at the request of the Pharisees and Sadducees. It would have been a waste of his time. (*Matthew 16:1-4*)

JESUS TRUSTED IN THE TIMING OF EVENTS

In going to Lazarus, Jesus trusted that the time was right. (*John 11:6, 40*)

JESUS ARGUED ABOUT TIMING

At Cana, with his mother,
he responded to her request,
"Dear woman, why do you involve
me? "My **time** has not yet come."
(*John 2:4*)

And yet he did as she asked in changing water to wine.

"After this, Jesus and his disciples went out into the Judean countryside, where he spent some time with them, and baptized." John 3:22

HE RECOGNIZED INTERRUPTIONS
AS DIVINE APPOINTMENTS

Jesus stopped on a busy day when someone reached out to touch him. (*Matthew 9:18-26*)

He stopped other activities and took time for children. (*Mark 10:13-16*)

JESUS UNDERSTOOD THAT PEOPLE HAVE CHOICE
OVER TIME

Even speaking of the day of rest, the Sabbath, Jesus gave it order and perspective.

Then he [Christ] said to them, "The Sabbath was made for man, not man for the Sabbath." Mark 2:27

God and Time

Day 1, God created light. This is a reminder of the light God sent into the world – Jesus. The Word itself is to be a light onto our path.

Begin days and tasks with the Word. This will enlighten your mind. It will give you direction in life.

Day 2, God separated the expanse of heaven from the waters below.

Sort out what is heavenly, of eternal value, and what is not.

Day 3, God separated the dry land from the water, and filled the earth with plants that could reproduce.

We need to fill our time with beauty and with what will grow. Our plans should include the ability to grow.

Day 4, God created the stars and planets, and used them to divide time into seasons, days, and years.

We need to divide our dreams and work for the future, understanding that each work has a season. All does not need to be done in one day.

Day 5, God created animals, birds, and fish, creatures that moved and reproduced. He created creatures that adapted over time.

We should work on what is fruitful, reproducible. Ask, "Can it go on and move in new directions after I start it? Can I pass it on to someone else?"

Day 6, God created man in his own image, to rule over the other creations of God. Only on this day did God state that his work was very good.

We have responsibility to care for what God made. We also should set models for others to follow. Helping others see the image of God within people and helping them connect to God is the Christian's goal.

Day 7, God rested. He stopped from his work and made the day special. He blessed the day of rest.

We, too, need rest. Too often over-committed people do not schedule rest and that leads to burnout. Rest from the creative process, too — don't spend the time dreaming and thinking of new ideas.

Making the most of time with God

If God is to be an integral part of your life then you need to share your time with him and let God be in control of your time.

Nehemiah was a man of prayer who listened.

He saw God speak through results and others.
(Nehemiah 2:18)
Nehemiah heard God in his heart. (Nehemiah 7:5)
He heard God speak in his mind. (Nehemiah 2:12)

Spending time with God means to talk with God and to listen to him.
The hard part is the listening.

Try POWER listening

Prayer As you pray, stop and listen for God to guide you with a conviction in your heart, an idea in your mind, or a quiet voice.

Other Christians Listen to wisdom of others.
Ask Christians to pray for you.
Ask a mature Christian to help you understand what you hear.

Word of God Read and reflect on God's Word. Find key ideas and principles in Scriptures to apply to your life.

Evaluation of circumstances
Evaluate events and opportunities to see what God is telling you through circumstances. Ask yourself
Did this happen after a certain prayer?
Do I have a passion for the circumstance?
Do I exhibit talent for this opportunity?
Does the opportunity match my mission and my talents?

Results Is there fruit from the labor? If so, God blessed the work.
If there is only frustration, ask God to show you why.
If there is no fruit, you may need to wait, nurture the activity, or stop doing it. Pray for wisdom.

Goal setting

Setting a goal is writing down a dream that you desire to attain.

Paul set and kept moving toward his goals

- ❀ Before ministering Paul prayed. *(Galatians 1:17)*
- ❀ He stayed focused on his goals. *(Philippians 3:14)*
- ❀ He prayed for God's direction. *(1 Thessalonians 5:17)*
- ❀ He pleased God instead of people. *(2 Corinthians 1:23)*
- ❀ He always chose to be content. *(Philippians 4:11)*
- ❀ His companions shared his goals. *(Acts 181-3, 18-22)*
- ❀ Problems and emergencies did not discourage Paul. *(Shipwreck, Acts 27; prison, Acts 16)*

WINNING IN THE GAME OF LIFE: A study of Harvard University graduates revealed one distinction of successful people: they wrote and posted goals.

TYPES OF GOALS

> Short term: daily, weekly goals
> Long term: yearly, lifetime
> Tangible: new business or ministry, special purchase
> Intangible: value development

MISSION STATEMENT

This is a brief explanation of your purpose in life (greatest desire to impact your world). Look at your goals and listen to God's direction to define your mission.

STEPS TO SETTING GOALS

- ❁ Pray.
- ❁ List plans you believe God has for your life.
- ❁ Assess your talents.
  List abilities, skills, and education.
- ❁ Access your resources.
  Money, time, supplies, and space available.
- ❁ Discover your passions.
  Choices if you could do anything.
  How would you spend free days?
  Activities you most enjoy.
  People you enjoy serving most.
- ❁ Dream BIG.
- ❁ Write a list of what you want
  to accomplish in life-each item
  is a goal.
- ❁ Write steps needed to attain
  each goal.

Set a yearly date to review and redefine your goals and mission statement.

POST YOUR GOALS

BE FLEXIBLE

Listen to God.
Listen to the wisdom of mature Christians.
Be willing to change plans.
Be content when plans fall short.
Evaluate yearly. Adjust goals if needed.

SAMPLE MISSION STATEMENTS

- ❁ To share God's love with at least one child daily.
- ❁ I want to do all I can to eliminate hunger in my
  community and in the world.

Evaluate your time

> "Be very careful, then, how you live–not as unwise but as wise, making the most of every opportunity, because the days are evil."
> Ephesians 5:15-16

It has been said that a woman can do everything–wife, mother, friends, ministry, and career – but not all at the same time.

Assess your current schedule. Knowing how you spend time can help you make wise future choices.

Record all your minutes for one week. Figure out how much time is spent in each area of your life. Some activities may involve more than one area.

- Household chores
- As a spouse
- Prayer and Bible study
- As a wife
- Bored or doing nothing
- Working/career
- Time with children
- Relaxing
- Volunteering
- Watching TV
- Hospitality at home
- Sleeping
- In a hobby
- As a daughter or sister
- Pleasure or play
- Eating
- As a friend
- Gossiping
- Interruptions
- Driving
- Waiting
- Planning
- Thinking
- Computer time

REVIEW THE LIST OPPOSITE

Put a red mark next to areas where time is wasted.
Star areas where time spent matches desires.
Put a green mark next to areas of neglect.
Put an X next to the least important activities.
Circle areas where time matches goals or mission.
Draw a heart next to all necessary activities.

ß

EXPLORE POSSIBILITIES

❋ Consider eliminating activities that don't move toward your goals or fulfill your mission.

❋ See what activities you can give up. Let people involved know you are making new time choices.

❋ Reflect on necessary activities, such as nurturing children. Remember it will pass.

❋ Look for spare moments to add activities. First, be sure you have the time and desire.

❋ Place some pursuits on hold for another season.

❋ Combine activities, such as running errands.

ß

3 STEPS TO TIME CHOICES

1. Determine urgency and necessity of tasks.
2. Prioritize tasks and group like chores.
3. Simplify. Eliminate the unimportant, non urgent.

ß

There is a time for everything, and a season for every activity under heaven: Ecclesiastes 3:1

Time considerations

When I planned this, did I do it lightly? Or do I make my plans in a worldly manner so that in the same breath I say, "Yes, yes" and "No, no"? 2 Corinthians 1:17

CONSIDERATIONS to reflect on before making a commitment of time
- ❀ Consider the cost
- ❀ Consider the motives
- ❀ Consider the importance
- ❀ Consider the need to be filled

OTHER FACTORS TO CONSIDER

Discover your strengths.

Discover your weaknesses.

What past activities brought joy?

What activities brought frustration?

Will this bring joy, satisfaction, or a sense of accomplishment?

Will this cause growth or build character?

℘

PRAY AND FOLLOW THESE STEPS IN TIME DECISIONS

1 List how this time commitment will glorify God and be in his will.
   If you cannot answer this, then say "No."

2 Ask, "How does this choice fit with my talents, goals, mission, and desires?"
   If it does not fit, consider declining unless it is to help you grow.

3 Name three other people who could do this activity. Does one of them have more time or need to do it more than you?
   Are you jealous and trying to lock out someone else? If so, say "No." Then pray and ask for forgiveness.

4 Ask, "Am I doing this to feel needed and am I really needed?"
   Decide if that is a good reason before making your decision.

Every time you say "No" you give someone else the opportunity to say "Yes."

Consider
the cost

"Suppose one of you wants to build a tower. Will he not first sit down and estimate the cost to see if he has enough money to complete it?" Luke 14:28

Consider the cost of your time before deciding how to spend it.

Ask the right questions before committing time, especially large portions of time

- ❀ What must I give up to make time for this?
- ❀ How will my commitment impact my family? Devotions?
- ❀ How long will I be obligated? Days? Weeks? Years?
- ❀ What is the eternal benefit of my doing this?
- ❀ Have I prayed about this? How has God answered?
- ❀ Does my family support this commitment?
- ❀ Who else will be involved?
- ❀ Am I really needed?
- ❀ How would my involvement benefit others?
- ❀ Is this the right time in my life for this?
- ❀ Does this commitment fit my personal, family, and ministry goals?
- ❀ Do I have a vision for this project? Do I have a passion and heart for it?
- ❀ What else will it cost? Money? Energy? Sacrifice?
- ❀ Is there flexibility to change my commitment later?

As a slave to a king, Nehemiah's
time was not his own. He chose
to work on a difficult project
rebuilding Jerusalem's walls and
people's relationship with God.
He set a time limit when the king
wisely asked him to do so.
Nehemiah spent twelve years on
the project, although the actual
reconstruction of the wall was
completed in fifty-two days.

*"Then the king, with the
queen sitting beside him,
asked me, "How long
will your journey take,
and when will you get
back?" It pleased the
king to send me; so I set
a time." Nehemiah* 2:6

SET LIMITS

- Consider how to train others and pass on the work.
- Set a time and a money limit and stick to it. Good
  stewardship is very important for your family.
- Set weekly limits. Tell your limits to the person
  enlisting you and when you reach those limits,
  remind the person you are stopping.
- Remember an expected small commitment may
  demand more time and energy than anticipated.
- Enlist help when you realize the cost is too great.

God gave you a family so include them in decisions.
  Before making any commitment, ask them

> Do you think this is a wise use of my time?
> Will you support my effort?
> Will you join me in doing it?
> If you are against it, will you explain why?
> What commitments to you do I need to keep?
> Will this activity interfere?

Respect and honor answers from loved ones.

Consider the motives

Paul changed his plans to go to Corinth. He
followed God's redirection and went to Macedonia.
Paul questioned his motives (worldly or according to
God's wisdom). Read 2 Corinthians 1:12-23.

*When I planned this, did I do it lightly? Or do I make my
plans in a worldly manner so that in the same breath I say,
"Yes, yes" and "No, no"?* 2 Corinthians 1:17

CONSIDER YOUR MOTIVES

Good reasons

> It is clearly God's will.
> It is my passion.
> It is an activity that includes my loved ones.
> It helps me grow and fits my goals and mission.

Bad reasons

> Selfish motives, such as, "I will gain if I do it."
> I will be the center of attention.
> I just can't say "No." to this person.
> I don't trust that anyone else can do it right.
> I will feel guilty if I say "No.".
> It gives me control or power.
> Desire to feel needed.

FIND THE MOTIVES

- For five minutes write why you might say "Yes."
- Discuss commitment with God, family, and friends.
- Divide a paper into two columns. In the left column write reasons to accept the commitment. In the right column write reasons to decline.
- Reread your mission statement and goals.

Stop to Pray
Ask your family's permission
Ask yourself if you have the time to give it your best.
Look at your calendar and available time.
Consider cost in time, energy, emotions, and resources.
Listen to God's response

GUILT DIFFUSERS

- Hug every family member.
- Ask God to heal what caused the guilt.
- Ask your family to express joy that you said "No."
- Believe God wants someone else to do it.
- Pray for those who committed to the activity.
- Reflect on Matthew 6:33-34

THREE STEPS TO WISE CHOICES

1. **Gather information.** Discover what is involved, pray, and figure out if you have the time and resources for it.

2. **Analyze.** Weigh pros and cons, and then decide.

3. **Apply/Evaluate.** Are you happy with your decision? How will it impact future commitments?

Consider the importance: prioritize

"but only one thing is needed. Mary has chosen what is better, and it will not be taken away from her." Luke 10:42

Life is full of momentary choices. In the famous Mary and Martha spat, Jesus pointed out that Mary made the better choice by sitting at his feet.

A **priority** is a prior or necessary time commitment.

KEEP YOUR LOVED ONES AND GOALS AS TOP PRIORITIES

Write your mission and goals on your calendar.
    Place a photo of your family on your calendar.

Before making a decision
    1. When asked to make a commitment, respond by stating you always pray first.
    2. Look at your calendar. Re-read the mission statement and ask, "Does this commitment fit?"
    3. Take a deep breath, look at your family photo and ask, "Is this commitment fair to my loved ones?"

Rank the following in importance

___ God	___ Peace of mind	___ Friends
___ Career	___ Feeling needed	___ A cause
___ Fun	___ A new project	___ Health
___ Family	___ Fame	___ Home

Now consider the new choice and see if it will interfere with the above ranking.

TRY IT

- ❀ Make your family a top priority for one day and see what harmony results.
- ❀ Schedule time with God and guard it. After one week, reflect on what difference it has made.
- ❀ Make relationships a priority. Look and listen with your heart, ears, and eyes.
- ❀ Eliminate unimportant activities as much as possible.
- ❀ Delegate responsibilities, even household chores.

LOSING SIGHT

Mary and Joseph lost Jesus! They knew he was God's Son and thus God's priority. Distraction cost time and worry. They turned around, left their traveling companions, and spent three days searching for Jesus. Then they had to return home. Joseph probably lost time from work and thus income.

Many family break-ups start with over-commitment and neglecting loved ones. Your child and spouse will remember your love and little acts of kindness more than any plaque earned from being on a committee or success at work.

Everyday let your VIPs know you care by your actions, words, and time given to them.

CHECKLIST FOR EACH PERSON YOU LOVE, INCLUDING GOD

___ I prayed for them.

___ I said, "I love you."

___ I did something for that person today.

___ I spent time with them today.

Saying "No" graciously

Jesus said "No." on several occasions.

NO MIRACLES TODAY BOYS!
In Matthew 12:38 and Mark 8:12 the Pharisees demanded a sign to test him. Jesus said "No.".

"NO" TO WORK, "YES" TO A RESTFUL BREAK
Jesus told his disciples to retreat when large crowds kept them too busy. *(Mark 6:30-31)*

"NO" TO MARTHA
When Martha complained, Jesus rebuked Martha, and said she worried about unimportant things. *(Luke 10:38-42)*

LET'S NOT RUSH. Consider the worst scenario.
When Mary and Martha sent for Jesus to heal Lazarus, Jesus waited. After all, the worst case scenario was death and Jesus had power over death. *(John 11:4-44)*

Before healing a child, Jesus stopped to heal a woman. *(Matthew 9:18-26)*

LESSONS FROM JESUS' EXAMPLE
- ❀ Do not waste time on wicked people.
- ❀ When life is hectic, pause and take a break.
- ❀ Say "No" to busyness.
- ❀ Don't rush to every crisis. Ask God for direction.

REASONS FOR "NO"

It does not fit your plans or goals.

You prayed and received no encouragement from God or received a "No."

It interferes with family relationships.

You have commitments or pressing deadlines.

Your spouse (or accountability buddy) said "No."

It wastes time (television, spam, frivolous phone calls or meetings). Eliminate these.

WAYS TO GRACIOUSLY SAY "NO." (IN MORE WAYS THAN ONE)

- I have other priorities so I must decline.
- I'm so over-committed I wouldn't do it justice.
- Let me suggest someone else.
- It is unfair to my family and others to whom I already made commitments.
- I cannot do it, but let's chat about how you can get the job done.
- If you can wait until I have more time I will get back to you.
- I am sure you care enough to understand I must say "No."
- I am honored that you would consider me, but I must decline.
- I simply do not have the resources or ability to do it.
- If I had the time I would love to. Is there any way you can help me with my other commitments?
- This is one of those times I am too overloaded.
- My dear family needs me. Surely you understand.
- My husband has other plans to occupy my time.

When to say "Yes"

Times Jesus said "Yes."

COMPASSION MOVED JESUS

In Matthew 14:14 and Mark 6:34 and 8:2, Jesus
responded to people's needs. He took time to teach,
heal, and even feed them.

FAITH AND PERSISTENCE MOVED JESUS

Matthew 8:5-13 and 15:22-28 show times when Jesus
responded to the great faith of someone and said
"Yes." to the requests.

JESUS SAID "YES." TO HIS FATHER'S WILL

In the garden of Gethsemane Jesus said "Yes." to God
over his own desires. He stated that he came to do his
Father's will and completed the task. *(John 4:34 and 17:4)*

JESUS SAID "YES." TO SUPPORT HIS HELPER

When Peter agreed that Jesus would pay taxes, Jesus
scolded Peter yet provided the money through a miracle.

DISCIPLES WHO SAID "YES."

- Mary said "Yes!" when God sent an angel.
- Stephen, said "Yes." to preaching and died for it.
- Peter said "Yes." to meeting with Cornelius
  because of a vision God gave him although it was
  contrary to his Jewish upbringing.
- Encountering Jesus changed Paul's goals. He
  learned to say "Yes." even when he had other
  plans. He let God use his weakness.

REASONS FOR SAYING "YES"

> God showed you he wants
>   you to commit to it.
> It is urgent and must be done.
> You have a passion for it.
> It will nurture your
>   relationships.
> You have the resources and
>   time available.
> Your family supports the decision.
> You have said, "No" to something else.
> Your compassion moves you to action.
> You do it to support your family.
> This is a more productive use of your time.

CHANGING POINTS IN LIFE WITH OPEN TIME

After a move, after children start school or leave home,
    or other transitions, you may have available time.
    Don't rush to fill the hours. Pray, and wait for God's
    answer. God may plan to give you a new ministry.

SAY "YES" BUT SET BOUNDARIES

- Qualify needs, i.e., "Yes, if you can supply workers
  or resources I will do it."
- Set boundaries. Limit the time or duration. State,
  "I will give one hour every Thursday." "I will do it
  this one year." Or "I can do it until school ends."
- State boundaries, such as "I expect you to find a
  music leader." Or, "I can help with the banquet but
  not the cleanup because of my children's bedtime."
- Schedule it, including prayer and prep time.
- Be prepared to keep your word and follow through.

Looking ahead

She is clothed with strength and dignity; she can laugh at the days to come. Proverbs 31:25

The proverbs woman laughed at the future! No wonder! She spent her time wisely. She cared for her family, helped the needy, ran a business, and invested in land.

Let today's decisions about time and priorities prepare you for the future.

ENVISION YOUR FUTURE

What do you think the Lord sees for your future?
Be willing to accept His plans.
What do you want it to look like?
Make choices that will help it happen.
Who do you want to share it with?
Love and serve those people now.

INVEST FOR TOMORROW

Investing time in people develops lasting relationships. Consider tithing time to God in ministry, for he calls us to be servants.

JESUS AND FUTURE PLANS

Jesus pointed out that the harvest is plenty but workers are few. (*Matthew 9:37*)

He sows love so we can reap souls.
Follow Christ's example of loving others. That's the

biggest step in taking part in the Great Commission. (*Matthew* 28:19-20)

Include sharing your faith in your future. Share faith with your children and other loved ones at every opportunity.
Be ready to share your faith with anyone you meet.

INVEST IN ETERNITY
Spend time with God daily.
Believe in Jesus as your Savior and as the Son of God.

Acts 16:31b ... *"Believe in the Lord Jesus, and you will be saved—you and your whole household."*

LOOKOUT FOR BUSY DAYS
Circle dates that are very busy, on your calendar.
Prepare for those dates. Here are a few suggestions.

- Pray.
- Let your family know why it will be a busy day and how they can help.
- Make and freeze meals for future use or buy ingredients for easy meals.
- Make a list of what is needed on that day. Fix or set aside items needed before the date, in a labeled box.
- Clean and do laundry before the date.
- Schedule yourself out of driving any carpools that day.
- The day before get extra rest or go to the beauty parlor and relax.

In Proverbs 6:6-11 and 30:25, God praised the wise ant that prepares for the future.

Accountability partner

Sometimes it takes two!
Jesus sent disciples out in pairs.
Paul and Timothy worked as friends,
travel companions, and accountability
partners.

*"As iron sharpens
iron, so one man
sharpens another."*
Proverbs 27:17

The word companion means someone
who breaks bread with another.
It describes a person who encourages
you and shares your relationship with
Jesus, the bread of life.

Find an accountability partner.
It may be your spouse, a friend, or family member.

QUALITIES OF AN ACCOUNTABILITY COMPANION:

Keeps confidences.

Listens to you.

Shares her problems and joys from her heart
honestly.

Prays for you and with you.

Encourages you.

Speaks truth with love.

Checks to be sure you keep to your goals and faith.

Can correct you in ways you can accept.

MEET WITH YOUR
ACCOUNTABILITY
PARTNER
You may set lunch
meetings, use
email, or phone to
stay in touch.
Listen to her.
Let her know your
prayer needs.

Or choose to have a more formal get-together such as
a "Pray and Plan." You may develop a routine or
agenda for formal meetings.

SAMPLE "PRAY AND PLAN"

- ❁ Keep a notebook of one another's goals/mission
  and prayer needs.
- ❁ Review progress on goals and answers to prayers.
- ❁ Pray and thank God for his answers and
  provisions.
- ❁ Bring up new ventures or possible time
  commitments.
- ❁ Pray over the possibilities and decisions.
  Silently listen for God's answers.
- ❁ Listen for wisdom God places in your mind.
  Note your partner's upcoming hectic days.
- ❁ Commit to pray for your partner's busy days.
  Pray for your partner, her goals, and God's
  direction for her.

Delegating

In Exodus, Moses faced burnout. Jethro, his father-in-law, spent one day observing all Moses did and noted that Moses micro-managed. He offered a simple solution: delegate work and responsibility. (*Exodus 18:1-27*)

A FAST SOLUTION THAT WORKS
Find reliable helpers.
Allot smaller tasks.
Solve the most difficult problems yourself.
Take time left for family.

If you are burning out and stressed from too much responsibility start delegating! Trust other people to do their part and know they will learn from mistakes. Be grateful for help without expecting perfection.

DELEGATE HOUSEHOLD TASKS
1. Take time to train the workers!
2. Write down all you think you can give away.
3. Meet with your family and divide the chores.
4. Keep the hardest tasks for yourself.

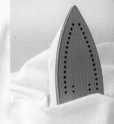

SAMPLE TASKS TO ASSIGN:

- Washing clothes
- Sorting and folding laundry
- Cleaning bathrooms
- Sweeping floors
- Pet care
- Vacuuming carpets
- Lawn care

In ministry, you can also delegate when your responsibility is too much to do alone. List every task you do and consider what you can give away and what you need to do.

RECRUITMENT SAVVY

- Break down the tasks to small ones.
- Describe responsibilities with boundaries and even meeting times so people will be more willing to commit.
- Praising people makes you easier to work with and garners more help.
- Try to find people to work together who are or can become friends.
- Look for people with talents you need but accept all offers of help.
- Match up people willing to do opposite tasks.
- Enlist those who can do smaller tasks to help busier leaders.
- Be a good listener and encourager for workers.
- Receive suggestions well and try to use any ideas offered by helpers.
- Be willing to help when emergencies arise.

Time and personality

The **popular/sanguine** personality is talkative, loud,
and expressive. People and fun are top priorities.
Calendars and deadlines may be lost or not checked.

TIME TIPS
- Ask people to give you reminders.
- Use a huge wall calendar with bright colored
  markers for appointments. Circle important dates.
- To be on time, write the time as 30 minutes earlier.
- Take time to listen to people.
- Limit your talking, especially when leading.
- Limit interruptions. When you begin preparing
  to leave let the answering machine handle calls.
- Sanguine Bible women: Miriam and Elizabeth.
- Helpful verse: Proverbs 25:11

The **powerful/choleric** personalities are busy people
who like facts, control, and leadership. They are
more interested in goals than people.

TIME TIPS
- Smile more. Be diplomatic and empathetic.
- When you lead, allow time for people to be late.
- Start meetings with social time. Greet people.
- Don't interrupt. Use input from others.
- Relax. Enjoy stories and jokes.

- Take time to say 'please' and 'thank-you'.
- Take time to appreciate others.
- Ask, instead of ordering, to motivate others.
- Powerful/choleric Bible women: Martha and Lydia.
- Helpful verse: Proverbs 16:24

Perfect/melancholy personality is quiet, detailed, and reserved. This thinker strives for perfection.

TIME TIPS

- Smile more. Laugh at yourself and problems.
- Don't get bogged down in details that waste time.
- Share your thoughts.
- Avoid over-analyzing people's words and actions.
- Take time to relax and be thankful.
- Forgive others who hurt your feelings.
- Perfect/melancholy Bible women: Dorcas and Esther.
- Helpful verse: 2 Thessalonians 3:16

Peacemaker/phlegmatics are easy-going, with a sense of humor. They strive for peace. They procrastinate.

TIME TIPS

- Take time to express joy.
- Get excited about things, especially gifts.
- Take the time to make decisions
- Express your opinions.
- Avoid procrastination. Give yourself deadlines.
- Take time to be discerning. Don't hold grudges.
- Actively participate in tasks and conversations.
- Peacemaker Bible women: Deborah and Priscilla.
- Helpful verse: James 1:22

Time and hospitality

In the familiar account of Mary and Martha, Mary chose to sit at the feet of Jesus and not be concerned about worldly needs. She may have finished her chores earlier but felt no obligation to help Martha.

Martha was not prepared for company and had a "help-me" self-centered attitude. She tried to manipulate Jesus and control Mary. Jesus pointed out that Mary made the wise choice. Mary had a guest-centered attitude.

DEVELOP A GUEST-CENTERED ATTITUDE

- Keep a space clean for impromptu entertaining.
- Consider spending time with friends as your priority.
- Let guests help if they offer.
- Spend time sitting and listening. Look at the person and listen with your eyes too. Don't interrupt.
- Allow overnight guests freedom to be comfortable. Show them where snacks and drinks are kept and laundry is done so they can help themselves. Allow them quiet time alone.

PREPARE FOR FUN

- Keep food items on hand that you can make easily. Make extra cookie dough and freeze it to slice and bake at a moment's notice.
- Keep enough for an extra meal on hand for unexpected company.
- Avoid procrastination so you will not be so pressured that you have to say "No." to fun opportunities.
- Smile when you speak on the phone – it actually relaxes your voice and the listener will feel more at ease.
- Schedule lunch dates with friends and special times with family.
- Learn a few jokes to share.
- Look at the light side of things and learn to laugh at yourself.

SOCIAL INTERACTION TIMING

Priscilla, a diplomatic friend and hostess, treated others well. She knew some secrets of good timing (*Acts 18*).

- She welcomed Paul to stay in her house, as a fellow tentmaker. As a fellow Christian worker she had time for unplanned company.
- When she found Apollos teaching inaccurately, she and her husband waited for an opportunity to correct him privately. She chose a good time to guide someone and did it discreetly.
- Paul called her a fellow worker. She gave time to ministry.
- She had time for family and ministered with her husband, Aquila.

Seven successful S's when overwhelmed

Some days are packed with activity or unexpected emergencies that bring great stress. Compressing too much into time is one cause of stress. Seek relief from stress.

- Scripture support
- Seek guidance
- Sort it out
- Simplify
- Schedule time periods
- Share the load
- Stop to relieve stress

Scripture support

LEARN AND REPEAT FAVORITE SCRIPTURES

In your car and home post Scriptures that help you
  overcome challenges.

SCRIPTURES ABOUT GOD'S POWER OVER TIME:

- He has made everything beautiful in its time.
  He has also set eternity in the hearts of men;
  yet they cannot fathom what God has done from
  beginning to end. *Ecclesiastes 3:11*
- Let us then approach the throne of grace with
  confidence, so that we may receive mercy and find
  grace to help us in our time of need. *Hebrews 4:16*
- And who knows but that you have come to royal
  position for such a time as this? *Esther 4:14b*
- My times are in your hands; deliver me from my
  enemies and from those who pursue me. *Psalm 31:15*
- No discipline seems pleasant at the time, but
  painful. Later on, however, it produces a harvest of
  righteousness and peace for those who have been
  trained by it. *Hebrews 12:11*
- The salvation of the righteous comes from the
  LORD; he is their stronghold in time of trouble.
  Psalm 37:39
- Let us not become weary in doing good, for at the
  proper time we will reap a harvest if we do not
  give up. *Galatians 6:9*

Seek guidance

Seek God
    Pray
    Read Scriptures.
    Journal after prayer and reading. Wisdom from
        God flows then.

&

Talk with your pastor
    Listen to his counsel.

&

Talk with your spouse or accountability partner
    Ask them to pray with and for you.
    Ask if they can lighten your load.
    Listen and follow advise.

&

Talk to a wise Christian friend, someone who
    will listen
    Talk and then listen.

Sort it out

LIST EVERY BURDEN THAT IS CAUSING STRESS
Look over the list and sort out thoughts and priorities

- Forgive anyone involved in the stress triggers.
- Circle the most urgent item and tackle that.
- Let go of the rest for the moment and focus on the urgent.
- Find activities on the list to eliminate or delegate and do so.
- Continue to do one thing on the list at a time.
- Do not take on any other activities until your stress is eased.

⌐

THE SORTING COMES DOWN TO ONE OF FOUR
    CHOICES for each item on the list
    Activities you must do.
    Activities you can eliminate.
    Activities you can put on hold.
    Activities you can delegate.

Simplify

SIMPLIFY YOUR HOME

Be less perfect.

Ask family members to do more.

Serve food on paper plates and wear no-iron clothes.

Make simple one-pot meals or sandwiches.

SIMPLIFY BY GROUPING

Group errands.

Set aside one block of time for all phone calls.

SIMPLIFY BY DIVISION

Divide big projects into steps.

Do one step at a time or delegate parts.

SIMPLIFY BY EASING YOUR MIND

Just think of one task at a time and focus on that.

Schedule time periods

BLOCK TIME FOR EACH MAJOR TASK
It may also help to assign tasks to different days.

ᴫᴽ

WORK ON THE ACTIVITY AT THE ASSIGNED TIME/DAY
Stop when time is up.

ᴫᴽ

USE SPARE MOMENTS FOR LITTLE TASKS
- Fold one basket of clothes.
- Make one quick call.
- Take frozen food out to thaw.
- Chop vegetables for dinner.
- Make your bed.
- Write a note.
- Clean one thing or small area.

Share the load

SHARE THE LOAD WITH GOD
Cast your cares on the LORD and he will sustain you;
he will never let the righteous fall. Psalm 55:22

SHARE THE LOAD WITH
LOVED ONES
- Enlist the family for meal preparation and chores.
- Enlist volunteers to help with your commitments.
- Ask for prayer support.

SHARE THE LOAD WITH OTHERS
- Let people in charge know you are having problems.
- Find substitutes for ministry and committees.
- Ask a friend to help you finish a project.
- Set up carpools.

SHARE THE LOAD WITH YOURSELF
- Take breaks.
- Prepare ahead.
- Agree to not be perfect.
- Forgive yourself for over-scheduling.
- Save mail and calls for the next day to focus on today's load.

Stop to relieve stress

RELIEVE THE PHYSICAL SYMPTOMS OF STRESS WITH
LITTLE BREAKS AND STRESS BUSTERS

- Take a walk.
- Breathe slowly and deeply, then let the air out slowly.
- Take a short nap.
- Laugh. Read jokes or watch a comedy show.
- Slowly sip a cup of tea.
- Chat with a friend who lifts you up.
- Read a short story or devotion.
- Listen to soft music.
- Soak in a hot tub.
- Exercise. It will produce hormones that make you feel better.
- Sit outside and look at God's creations.
- Eat a healthy snack.
- Read how someone with similar problems found solutions. This is called bibliotherapy.
- Massage your face and the back of your neck.

Overcoming procrastination

Still another said, "I will follow you, Lord; but first let me go back and say good bye to my family." Jesus replied, "No one who puts his hand to the plow and looks back is fit for service in the kingdom of God." Luke 9:61-62

Jesus criticized people who procrastinated on God's call, urging them to immediate action. Procrastination whittles away time yet accomplishes nothing.

TWO TYPES OF PROCRASTINATORS
- Stressed-out or worriers.
- Relaxed people, enjoying life but avoiding work.

TIPS FOR OVERCOMING COMMON EXCUSES
- Self-doubt – list past success, post mottos, and give yourself pep talks. If efforts fail re-evaluate skills, choose new activities, and seek advice.
- Self-degradation – accept compliments; appraise your worth in God's eyes.
- Perfectionism – lower expectations and standards, praise yourself as you work on the project.
- Defeatist attitude/fear of failure/what others will think – look to God not people. Focus on needs you can meet. List past successes.
- Disagreeable tasks – just do it and get it over with.
- Guilt – forgive yourself and get started.
- Hostility/anger – forgive. Let go of control.

❀ Overwhelmed – break project into parts.
Focus on one part at a time. Delegate some parts.

❀ Lack of skill/supplies – seek help, training and funding.

❀ Stalled – brainstorm. Ask for help.

❀ False sense of timing – realistically evaluate time
needed for job. Learn to time your activities.

❀ Priority is low – set a date/time to do it.

❀ Boredom – set a reward for doing it and
consequences for not doing it.

❀ Pleasure seeking – give yourself small rewards for
completing small parts.

❀ Habitual procrastinator – tackle one task at a time
and start a new habit of doing. Ask an
accountability partner for encouragement.

❀ Set up a distraction free work area. Lock yourself in.

❀ Forgetfulness – write it down and post it.

❀ Depression or other medical problem – seek
professional help. Give project away.

❀ Disorganized – gather everything needed for the
project and set up a task center.

❀ Desire to socialize instead – work in a team.

❀ Interdependency (fear it will affect a relationship) –
discuss this with people involved and pray about it.

❀ Fear of becoming workaholic – schedule fun and
set boundaries.

❀ Dreams of escape – be realistic. Face the project.

❀ Lack of interest/motivation – talk to others to
stimulate interest. List benefits of doing it.

❀ Crisis-maker – waiting causes a crisis that brings
attention. Seek other ways to be noticed.

POST SLOGANS AND GIVE YOURSELF PEP TALKS,
BUT DO IT!

Balancing time

> *"She [Deborah] held court under the Palm of Deborah between Ramah and Bethel in the hill country of Ephraim, and the Israelites came to her to have their disputes decided." Judges 4:5*

Deborah achieved balance by multitasking. She worked under a tree giving her time in the fresh air while working. Although she had a family and tried to stay home she agreed to travel with the Israelite army when requested.

BALANCE

People speak of balance in life and time. Women need a daily balance but a life with balance is more important. There are seasons of the year and seasons in life.

Jesus also sought to do more than one thing. He taught, healed, ate with friends, served others, and spent lots of time in prayer.

Review how you spend time and consider what areas are too hectic and what areas are neglected. Then work on rearranging your days to relieve stress and give time to things too often overlooked. Also consider your natural rhythm and what time of day you work best. Shift difficult tasks to that time.

CHECKLIST of areas you need to balance by lessening or increasing time spent:

- ☐ God (prayer, devotions, ministry)
- ☐ Relationships (spouse, children, friends, small group members, associates)
- ☐ Home (homemaking, family time, nurturing, hospitality)
- ☐ Work (career, education, deadlines)
- ☐ Self-care (relaxation, exercise, sleep, play)
- ☐ Growth (hobbies, skills, education, knowledge, spiritual growth)

Each area will have sub-lists, such as names of people under relationships. This is not a detailed list but an overview of how you spend time. Some areas will consume more time at different periods in your life, such as child rearing while you have little ones at home. If there is a big hole or an area that takes too much time consider what changes to make in the near future.

"Too tired" syndrome

Then he returned to his disciples and found them sleeping. "Could you men not keep watch with me for one hour?" he asked Peter. Matthew 26:40

In the garden the night before the Lord's death the disciples could not keep their eyes open no matter how much Jesus pleaded with them. Everyone has times of being exhausted and extremely tired.

If the tiredness continues for days, it is a signal that changes are needed or that you may need a medical check-up.

CAUSES AND SUGGESTED SOLUTIONS

Newborns and young children that drain energy:
Rest when your baby rests. Try not to nap, simply sit and relax.
Join a babysitting coop to give yourself a break.
Hire a mother's helper, even if only for one hour a day.

℘

Medical/body changes may need a doctor's care:
Hormone changes during pre-menopause/menopause
Thyroid problems, heart problems, and depression
Prolonged insomnia

℘

Insomnia:

Use the time to pray and let prayer help you
   unwind and relax.

Cut down on television. It stimulates the mind and
   inhibits rest.

Exercise more, but at least four hours before bedtime.

Keep your bedroom off limits except for sleeping.

Have a set bedtime and rising time.

Do light stretching before bed to relax muscles.

A lavender sachet under your pillow may help.

Warm milk releases tryptophan that aids sleeping.

Avoid chocolate and other caffeine foods/drinks
   at night.

ℬ

Busy schedule and driving children to activities:

Try to carpool or share driving with your spouse.

Relax while driving by listening to calming music.

Take rest breaks during the day to de-stimulate
   your body.

ℬ

Worry:

Pray and journal about problems and worries.

Then praise God.

Realize that you cannot change things before the
   next morning.

Note one thing to do about the problem
   tomorrow then sleep.

Ask a friend to pray for you including prayer that
   you can sleep.

ℬ

Interruptions, disruptions, and divine appointments

At once Jesus realized that power had gone out from him. He turned around in the crowd and asked, "Who touched my clothes?" Mark 5:30

A woman who touched the cloak of Jesus caused him to stop. Her faith also touched his heart and the interruption provided an opportunity for Jesus to talk about faith. It became a God moment or what some label as a divine appointment.

INTERRUPTIONS OR GOD INTERVENTIONS

Adjust your attitude about interruptions.

Pray for wisdom.

Pause to ask, "Is this an opportunity for God to use me?"

Smile when interrupted and try to deal with it calmly but firmly.

Consider that people are more important than schedules.

B'

DISRUPTIONS

Cope with recurring disruptions.

Screen or delay calls by using your answering machine and caller ID.

Consider ways to eliminate problems that recur.

Set times for calls and ask people to phone during that time.

Let family members know how to handle things without interrupting you.

℞

RECOGNIZE NEEDS

Realize that when children keep interrupting they are cries for attention.

Stop what you are doing and pay attention.

A few minutes of attention will generate peace and stretches of calm.

Children may be bored and need guidance/direction.

A friend may be in crisis but not opening up. Listen for cues in her voice.

℞

EMERGENCIES

Keep emergency numbers near the phone.

Have a few people you can call to help in emergencies.

Breathe deep and slow, then focus on what needs to be done first.

℞

Time wasters

TOP TIME WASTERS:

1. Procrastination
2. Worry
3. Running errands
4. Rushing
5. Telephone, mail, and email
6. Gossip
7. Paperwork, reports, and memos
8. Meetings
9. Television
10. Planning and decision-making
11. Internet surfing
12. Saying "Yes" when you want to say "No"

THE 20-80 RULE

On average, 80% of accomplishments are done in 20% of a person's time. In wasting less time, much more can be accomplished.

TIPS TO STOP WASTING TIME

1. Do things right away or set a date and stick to it.
2. Give the problem to God.
3. Group errands, order by phone and Internet.

Set aside one day a week for errands and plan the most efficient route.

4. Slow down and do things right.

5. Stop interruptions:

   ❁ Eliminate solicitors by getting on the "No call list."

   ❁ Open mail by the trash and immediately deal with whatever you do not toss.

   ❁ Don't open spam email. Delete it. Check email once or twice a day.

6. Stop gossiping or listening to it.

7. Handle papers FAST:

   ❁ File documents and important information.

   ❁ Act on bills and current information now.

   ❁ Store in a "Weekly to do" folder papers that need more information.

   ❁ Toss out everything else.

8. Ask for meeting agendas and only go if you are in charge or there is an item of interest on the agenda. Don't schedule meetings without a reason.

9. TV – limit yourself to 1-2 hours daily. Record shows you really want to see and fast forward through commercials.

10. Gather all info before making plans or decisions and then once gathered, make an informed decision.

11. Find a good search engine and learn to type in specific requests for information. Keep a list in your computer of favorites and use it to find information quickly.

12. Learn to say "No."

Family time

Impress them on your children. Talk about them when you sit at home and when you walk along the road, when you lie down and when you get up. Deuteronomy 6:7

God's instruction to parents reveals an expectation of spending time together as family. Time to sit, rest, walk, and waking up that is spent together.

More and more studies show that the biggest factor for good grades and preventing teen problems is eating meals together at least five days every week.

FAMILY MEALS

Write a menu and shop/prepare meals ahead.
Let everyone help set the table, cook, and cleanup.
Take turns or divide meal chores.
Turn off television and other distractions.
Begin with grace.
Chat about each person's day.
Discuss homework, tests, and school events.
Talk about joys and reasons to be thankful.
Share memories and jokes.

SPOUSE TIME

Set a date with your spouse at least once a month.
Pray together.
Join a couples Bible study.
Set time to discuss parenting, budget, and your relationship.

MAKE FAMILY A PRIORITY

Go to work earlier if needed, but arrive home for meals.
Schedule family outings and game nights.
Plan family trips and vacations together.

FAMILY MEETINGS

Meet together to pray and discuss problems or changes.
Focus on only one problem for each person.
Use meetings to praise family members too!
Discuss responsibilities, chores, and schoolwork.

FAMILY DEVOTIONS

Spend time together in God's Word.
Make it fun. Do an activity and then relate it to a Bible passage or verse.
Buy fun resources, such as Family Devotional Builders (Hendrickson Publishing)

TIMELY LESSONS

Help your children learn to gauge their time.
Explain that being on time is courteous.
Help your children make wise time choices.
Be a good role model of using time wisely.

FAMILY FUN

Try some of these activities for fun
Look through family photos or videos.
Picnic outdoors. Or picnic inside in bad weather.
Play board games.
Play ball.
Sing or dance.
Bicycle together.
Take a family walk.
Make ice cream sundaes.
Have a treasure hunt.

Timely home management

> "Suppose one of you wants to build a tower. Will he not first sit down and estimate the cost to see if he has enough money to complete it? For if he lays the foundation and is not able to finish it, everyone who sees it will ridicule him." Luke 14:28-29

Set schedules that can be finished during time available
Set a household-cleaning plan.
Organize your home so you can tidy it in minutes each morning.
Clean up right after meals.
Keep the family in tune with the plan.
Assign chores and consequences for undone chores.

ORGANIZATION

Families waste the most time searching for lost items and papers. Teach everyone to replace items after using them.

Organize paperwork:

- ❧ Set up folders and file papers regularly.
- ❧ Set up an area for bills and pay at once or on a set schedule.
- ❧ Set up a file for papers that you must work on and keep them together.
- ❧ Shred unneeded papers containing personal information.
- ❧ Toss or recycle all other unneeded papers.
- ❧ Try online or automatic payments.

RESOURCES

The Messies Manual by Sandra Felton (Revell Books)

More Hours in My Day by Emilie Barnes (Harvest House Publishers)

Making Your Home a Haven by Cindy Salzman (Christian Publications)

FINANCES

Managing a home works best with a spending and savings plan. Here are some basic guidelines:

- List all donations and monthly bills (mortgage, utilities, insurance, groceries)
- List any debts (credit card, car loans, student loans, children's activities, child care).
- Tithe first.
- Set aside enough to meet bills and pay down debt.
- Set aside money (up to 10%) for savings and emergencies.
- Do not spend more than you earn.
- Consider how to spend what is left (vacations, holidays, movies, dining out, clothes, etc.).
- Check interest rates and refinance for lower rates if feasible.
- Look for hidden costs.

RESOURCES

Debt proof Your Marriage by Mary Hunt (Revell)

The World's Easiest Guide to Finances by Larry Burkett, Randy Southern (Moody Publishers)

Avoid time crunches on special days

What will you do on the day of your appointed feasts, on the festival days of the Lord? Hosea 9:5

KEEPING CHRIST IN THE HOLIDAY

- ❁ Read Bible accounts before the holiday.
- ❁ For secular days, choose a virtue associated with the holiday and read Bible verses on it. For example, read about leadership qualities for President's Day.
- ❁ Use the decorations you have to chat about Jesus.
  - ❁ Valentines and other greeting cards can be opportunities to share the message of God's love.
  - ❁ Discuss contents of Easter eggs as symbols of joy and life.
  - ❁ Compare filling stockings with being filled with God's love.
- ❁ Talk about wreaths as signs of God's eternal love.
- ❁ Use holiday lights as reminders of Jesus as the light of the world and our being lights by reflecting God's love.
- ❁ Choose one project for the needy, such as the angel Christmas tree or making Easter tray favors for nursing home residents.

REMEMBERING SPECIAL DATES

- ❁ Buy a folder and fill it with cards and stamps. Keep a list of dates in the folder and check it before the beginning of each month.
- ❁ In January fill in special dates on a calendar.

GIFTS

◌ Simplify gift giving. Set up for groups to draw a name and thus buy one gift only. Or, buy a family gift rather one for each person.

◌ Wrap and label presents as purchased so gift-wrapping does not become stressful.

◌ Use gift bags instead of wrapping paper.

FOOD

◌ Join or set up cookie swaps to cut down on baking.

◌ Make and freeze foods ahead of time.

◌ For young families, consider setting out appetizers throughout the day instead of a sit down dinner.

◌ Bake a roast on time bake or in a roasting bag.

DECORATIONS

◌ Simple can be elegant and easy. A holiday wreath, simple centerpiece, and balloons can go a long way to making a place look festive!

◌ Store decorations in plastic tubs of colors associated with the holiday to make finding them easier.

SOCIALIZING

◌ Keep entertaining simple.

◌ Consider a tea or evening potluck dessert time rather than a dinner.

◌ Keep your invitation list short.

◌ Entertain out instead of at home.

PARTIES AND FUNCTIONS

◌ Check your family schedules and choose which parties will fit. Say "No." to others.

◌ Buy a basic outfit and change scarves/accessories to fit the holiday.

◌ Mark children's extra functions on the calendar, too. Limit each child's social activities.

Time for joy

An attitude of gratitude fills the heart with joy as does laughter.

You have made known to me the path of life; you will fill me with joy in your presence. Proverbs 16:11b

ADD SPLASHES OF JOY IN LITTLE MOMENTS

- ❀ Each morning thank God for the day and his presence.
- ❀ Spend daily time reading God's Word.
- ❀ Create a gratitude list of blessings in your life. Read and add to it once a week.
- ❀ Listen to uplifting music.
- ❀ Add humor to life with reading, TV, or joke books.
- ❀ Make bath time special with candlelight, fragrant new soaps, or music.
- ❀ Pray outside.
- ❀ Watch a sunrise or sunset.
- ❀ Walk outdoors and stop to smell the flowers.
- ❀ Snuggle up with a Christian book.

SPRINKLE OTHERS WITH JOY AND YOU WILL BE SHOWERED WITH JOY

- ❧ Compliment others.
- ❧ Lavish loved ones with hugs.
- ❧ Serve others in little ways: make favorite meals, do chores, or write encouraging notes.
- ❧ Spend distraction-free time with loved ones.
- ❧ Plan and hold a girl fun time with friends.
- ❧ Volunteer one hour for needy people.
- ❧ Cuddle with a loved one.
- ❧ With friends, sit by a fire or glowing candles.
- ❧ Send cards to friends.
- ❧ Call a friend to say hello.
- ❧ Call and share your joy with a friend.

"Your love has given me great joy and encouragement, because you, brother, have refreshed the hearts of the saints." Philemon 1:7

Timely Scriptures

GOD CREATED AND OWNS TIME
Daniel 2:21, Ecclesiastes 3:17, Ecclesiastes 8:8,
Job 39:1-2; 42:2, Matthew 24:36, 2 Peter 3:9,
Revelation 3:10

GOD'S PROMISES CONCERNING TIME
Isaiah 33:6, Isaiah 64:4, Joel 2:25, Matthew 10:19,
Acts 3:21, Ephesians 6:2-3, Hebrews 12:11

COMFORT FOR HARD TIMES
Psalm 9:9, Psalm 30:5, Psalm 37:39, Psalm 41:1,
Ecclesiastes 7:14, Ecclesiastes 8:6, Isaiah 33:2,
John 16:22

FUTURE TIME
Isaiah 9:7, Isaiah 30:26, Daniel 12:9, Habakkuk 2:3,
Mark 13:26, Luke 21:8, Romans 8:18, 1 Corinthians 4:5

TIME AND WORK
Proverbs 6:6-8, Proverbs 20:4, Proverbs 31:10-31,
Ecclesiastes 2:24, 1 Corinthians 15:58,
2 Corinthians 9:8, Galatians 6:9, James 4:13-15

OTHER USE OF TIME
Psalm 62:8, Proverbs 15:23, Ecclesiastes 8:5,
Amos 5:13, Matthew 6:27, John 4:23, Acts 3:19,
Colossians 4:5